Count Your Way through

Germany

by Jim Haskins

illustrations by Helen Byers

Carolrhoda Books, Inc./Minneapolis

To Brenan and Banyon. —J.H.

For Christopher and Kate. — H.B.

The cover illustration depicts the annual reenactment of the Pied Piper Legend in the town of Hameln, West Germany, during their Pied Piper festival.

LIBRARY OF CONGRESS CATALOGING-IN-PUBLICATION DATA

Haskins, Jim, 1941-
   Count your way through Germany/by Jim Haskins; illustrations by
Helen Byers.
      p.   cm.
   Summary: Uses the numbers one through ten in German to introduce
aspects of the history and culture of Germany.
   ISBN 0-87614-407-5 (lib. bdg.)
   1. Germany—Civilization—Juvenile literature. 2. German
language—Numerals—Juvenile literature. 3. Counting—Juvenile
literature. [1. Germany. 2. Counting.] I. Byers, Helen, ill.
II. Title.
DD17.H37   1990
943—dc20
[E]   89-22232
                                                          CIP
                                                           AC

Manufactured in the United States of America

1 2 3 4 5 6 7 8 9 10 99 98 97 96 95 94 93 92 91 90

Introductory Note

The German language comes from the same roots as English. Both developed from the prehistoric tongue called Indo-European, and there are many similarities between the two languages.

Many German words are spelled the same way in English, but they are pronounced differently. Examples are arm, hand, winter, and gold. Some German words are spelled differently than their English counterparts, but when they are spoken they sound similar. Examples are Vater (FAH-ter), which means father, Mutter (MUH-ter), which means mother, and Haus (howse), which means house.

German and English differ greatly, however, in the way sentences are put together. In German, the verb is often at the end of the sentence. For English speakers, it's hard to wait until the end of a sentence to find out what action is being described. German also has an accent mark that is unfamiliar to English-speakers, the double dot, or umlaut (¨). The only time it occurs in the numbers 1 through 10 is in the number 5. The umlaut makes the u sound something like the u in put.

1 eins (eyns)

Germany is **one** land divided into two nations. To the west is the Federal Republic of Germany (West Germany). To the east is the German Democratic Republic (East Germany). The division came about at the end of World War II, when Germany was defeated by a group of allied nations that included the United States, the Soviet Union, France, and Great Britain. The Allies could not agree on Germany's future, so it was divided. The area controlled by the Western powers became West Germany and the Soviet-controlled zone became East Germany.

For centuries, Germany was divided into many states. In fact, it did not become one nation until 1871. So, German people don't find this latest division of the land all that strange. But many hope that one day their country will be reunited.

Atlantic
Ocean

North
Sea

Baltic Sea

East
Germany

West
Germany

Mediterranean
Sea

Adriatic Sea

2 zwei (tsvy)

The Holsten Gate, the main entrance to Lübeck, has **two** conical towers. Built in 1477, the gate is the proud symbol of this 1,000-year-old city. During the Middle Ages, Germany was made up of dozens of separately governed regions, and each ruling family needed a stronghold to protect their land. Many of the gates and walls surrounding German cities were built to protect the inhabitants from enemy attacks.

3 drei (dry)

Three of the world's most famous composers of music are German. Johann Sebastian Bach (1685-1750) played the organ and during his lifetime was better known as an organist than as a composer. Ludwig von Beethoven (1770-1827) was a pianist and showed great talent even as a child. Today, his symphonies and concertos are played by the greatest pianists. Johannes Brahms (1833-1897) is most famous for his symphonies and concertos. In addition, Brahms's *Lullaby* is the most popular lullaby sung to children in the United States today.

4   **vier (feer)**

Four candles are placed on the traditional Advent wreath that is put up in many German homes in late November. The branches of the wreath are entwined with bright red ribbons, and it is either suspended from a chandelier in the living room or placed on a table. Advent is the four weeks before Christmas. Each Sunday the family gathers around the wreath and lights one candle for each week.

Many Christmas customs in the United States are similar to those practiced in Germany. Our Santa Claus has his counterpart in the German St. Nicholas. On December 6, German children put one of their shoes on the fireplace or windowsill, hoping that when they awaken the next morning, St. Nicholas will have filled it with goodies.

5 fünf (fuenf)

Five sights that you will see in the *Karneval* (kahr-neh-VAHL) parade are: huge floats, bands, funny groups of jesters wearing comical masks, and the Prince and Princess of the parade.

Karneval in the Catholic areas of Germany is much like Carnival in other parts of the world, including Mardi Gras in New Orleans. It is the time of feasting and pleasure before Lent. There is much fun during Karneval, but it is a lot of work for its organizers. They hold their first meeting at 11 minutes after 11 p.m. on the 11th day of the 11th month (November), and they work hard until Karneval begins in the spring.

6 sechs (zekhs)

Six popular breeds of dogs that originated in Germany are the poodle, schnauzer, German shepherd, Doberman pinscher, Great Dane, and dachshund.

While most dogs are kept as pets today, many were originally bred to do a specific kind of work. For instance, the dachshund was used to hunt small animals such as the badger, which it could pursue right down into the animal's narrow burrow. The poodle's name comes from the German word for "puddlers," or water dogs, because they retrieved ducks and other game from water for hunters. The schnauzer was trained to kill rats and to herd cattle and sheep. German shepherds were also bred to tend sheep. In the 1500s, the Great Dane, one of the largest of all dogs, served as a guard dog. Three hundred years later, Ludwig Dobermann bred the Doberman pinscher to be a smaller, but still fierce-looking, guard dog.

7 sieben (ZEE-ben)

Seven dwarfs are Snow White's friends in the famous folktale from Germany. It was first published by two German brothers, Jacob and Wilhelm Grimm. People had been telling the story for many years before it was written down. The legend comes from the Hesse region of Germany, where there are seven hills in which Snow White was said to have hidden.

The Brothers Grimm also published such tales as *Hansel and Gretel* and *Sleeping Beauty*. A great number of folktales and fairy tales well known to American children originated in Germany.

8 acht (ahkht)

The German Autobahn, or highway, has as many as **eight** lanes in urban areas. Even in the countryside, the autobahn is four lanes wide, so touring the country by car is easy throughout scenic Germany. Cars travel quickly on the autobahn because there are no speed limits. In most places, drivers can go as fast as they want. That's probably one reason some of the best and fastest cars in the world are made in Germany.

9 neun (noyn)

German **nine**-pin bowling, or *Kegeln* (KEH-geln), resembles the American game of ten-pin bowling except kegeln uses one less pin. Bowling has been played in Germany for centuries. Legend has it that American ten-pin bowling was developed as a way to get around the laws in colonial times that forbade the traditional German game of nine-pin bowling on Sundays.

Other popular sports in Germany include soccer, hiking, mountain climbing, and winter sports like skiing and skating.

10 zehn (tsehn)

There are **ten** feathers on the wings of the eagle that is the symbol of the Federal Republic of Germany (West Germany). The black eagle with red beak and talons is a very old symbol in Germany, dating back to the time when Germany was part of the Holy Roman Empire. When Germany was unified in 1871, the eagle became the symbol of a united Germany. When Germany was divided after World War II, the symbol of the eagle was kept by West Germany.

Pronunciation Guide

1 / **eins** / (eyns)

2 / **zwei** / (tsvy)

3 / **drei** / (dry)

4 / **vier** / (feer)

5 / **fünf** / (fuenf)

6 / **sechs** / (zekhs)

7 / **sieben** / (ZEE-ben)

8 / **acht** / (ahkht)

9 / **neun** / (noyn)

10 / **zehn** / (tsehn)